TRIPTI SHARMA

First Published in June 2022

ISBN: 978-93-5628-416-6

BLUEROSE PUBLISHERS

www.bluerosepublishers.com

info@bluerosepublishers.com

+91 8882 898 898

Cover Design:

Shreya Kapoor

Typographic Design:

Pooja Sharma

Distributed by: BlueRose, Amazon, Flipkart

Dedication

To lovers of Chrysalis

I believe this book helps you to connect to various series of emotions. Moreover, it will be able to capture the hearts and minds of the audience reading this book versatilely.

I would be grateful enough to see this book in every hand of people everywhere-audience of all generations will be able to link their notions with my write-up.

I am fortunate to take this as a challenge that can be futile but undoubtedly won't be worthless.

At your convenience, enjoy reading it.

The only recommendation I can make.

Preface

Poem composition is an art that helps to furnish feelings magnificently that isn't easy to express. I found it challenging to adapt to my life's changes to my vague remembrance post-pregnancy. I was unable to define and recognize my thoughts and emotions. At that point, I started writing my feelings on paper, which turned out into remarkable and beautiful compositions. My writing journey was captivating because of my deep-rooted opinions, expressions, and analysis of life's paradoxical experiences.

The articulated write-ups contain many emotions that will gracefully entice the reader's soul.

Acknowledgment

At the outset, I convey my profound, heartfelt gratitude to my role model and inspiration, Dr. Pradeep Siwach, Pro-Vice-Chancellor, Chitkara University, Rajpura, Punjab. He holds a prominent place in giving shape to my writing work. His consistent recognition, counseling, and encouragement played a pivotal role in the publication of this book.

I am also grateful to my tutor Hitesh Sachdev who motivated me to trust my writing skills. His sense of acknowledgment towards my poems enormously helped me make my dream come true.

My family outstandingly stood as a backbone in cherishing my composition and its publication. Their immense support gave wings to my passion for writing.

I wholeheartedly thank my readers and every individual who took the time to read my poems and appreciated my work.

Introduction

Chrysalis is a collection of short poems exquisitely appended into a series of emotions. The author precisely articulates all verses. In addition, the lyrics compilation caters to the feelings of all age groups. One of the striking features of this book is that its readers will be able to connect and find every poem amazingly relatable to one's life and situations. Another noteworthy aspect of this book is that every poem is soul-stirring and inspiring, which would undoubtedly fascinate the readers to their heart's core. The author has magnificently described every poem with deep emotions capturing the heart of every reader. Every verse of the poem is founded on the author's real-life experience. The writer has eminently coherent lyrics, straight from the heart. Nevertheless, these compositions will conquer reviewers' hearts, minds, and souls. The only wish of the author is to authenticate the feelings of the book reader and establish an exquisite connection with them through wordplay.

Contents

1. Mother's Demise 1
2. Deep Inside My Soul 3
3. It Happened 4
4. Your Silence 5
5. A Closed Door 7
6. Mind, Heart and Soul 8
7. Oh God, I Was A Child 9
8. Soulmate 11
9. Imperfections 12
10. A Broken Soul with Two Faces 13
11. Twinkle of Your Love 15
12. Transformation 16
13. Conviction 17
14. Human Relationships 18
15. Colour Box 20
16. Scattered Pieces 21
17. Belief... 22
18. I Set My Heart on Fire 23
19. Ph.D. Guide 24
20. Journey of My Flight 25

21. Havoc 26
22. Things Will Never Be Alright 27
23. Fades 28
24. Silent Battle 30
25. Twin Flame 32
26. No Point to Return Back 34
27. A Sound of Silence 35
28. Virus Outbreak 36
29. Soul Sister 38
30. Not Taking A Moment To Say Goodbye 39
31. Move On 40
32. Light Lamp 42
33. Last Breath 43
34. A Happy Land 45
35. Cosmic Connection 46
36. Happiness A Myth 47
37. Walk Without A Soul 48
38. Dreamful Life 49
39. A Man with Advice 50

1. Mother's Demise

I was a free bird when I was a child

My mother took my tension. And I wanted to fly

I was the naughtiest one; my siblings were quite

My mother was strict with me, but I did things that she always denied.

Writing and learning notes was monotonous to me

I hardly took my studies seriously

Books were never my friend, and it was a plight

As I was a free bird when I was a child

My ability to connect with stars, the moon, and sunshine was my pride

But my mother used to be angry at my acts, as I used to cross limits that she specified

Playing in the mud and splashing water made me gracious

And yes, my paper boat didn't ever sink in the rainwater as it had a spirit never to say die

Flowers, bird's nests, and of course, butterfly

Used to make me glorified

The collection of coins and marble brought vivacity to my life

I magnificently lived my childhood days.But today, I miss my mother's emotions and scoldings because she eventually died

Hey, once my mother took tension, and I wanted to fly, but her demise hijacked my flight.

2. Deep Inside My Soul

Deep inside my soul, there is a world waiting for you.

Now I will be alone in my painful and shattered life, and you will never hold me again.

Still, my world is waiting for you.

Ways of our togetherness have been lost. Now, our life's directions are different.

Still, my world is waiting for you.

Time has changed, the situation has changed, and our feelings have changed with this truth.

Still, my world is waiting for you.

You have left me forever with this heart-breaking fact by hurting each other to an extreme.

Still, my world is waiting for you.

Deep inside your soul, I know there is a world full of reactions for me never shown.

Still, my world is waiting for you.

3. It Happened

When the whole world was busy, I thought no one would feel my pain, and silent tears

It happened; I lost you, dear

When I thought I would not disturb you with my anger, expectations, and stupid nature

But It happened; I lost you, dear

When there was the exchange of sorry and care, I thought these special moments would not bring tears

But It happened; I lost you, dear

When there was a firm determination in my heart, whatever may happen, I would not lose you with a little bit of fear

But It happened; I lost you, dear.

4. Your Silence

Waiting was hard

The level of my hope was vast

But the magnitude of my patience was becoming significantly low

Replies from your side were slow

Something was making us apart

It was your silence

The number of questions in my mind were more

I don't remember you founding any sense in them for sure

My insecurities for you were becoming loud in fear.

But this stupidity of mine was not allowed; you were clear

One thing that maturely gave me all answers

Was your silence

Understanding everything is required

Sometimes having the conversation to explain things made you tried

My melted heart was broken into tiny pieces

You never uttered any words which were needed

As you had a powerful tool to disclose things

Was by your silence

My thoughts were becoming my weakness.

Being aware of my mistakes was making me helpless
I wanted things to get calm down
But you already made an effort for peace; I found
It was by your silence.

5. A Closed Door

There was a door between both of us, which made us apart

Positive energy and love used to flow from both sides

But in misconceptions, this door has been once closed from your side

Misunderstandings, ego, and assumptions captured space in your heart

You never attempted to clear that path

With self-motive, you closed that door

My side was clear to pass care and concern

Your recognition to consider my efforts was uncertain

Disregarding my deep feelings, you closed that imaginary door

As the door is locked from your side, I several times knocked on that door with the hope of getting things alright

I only have a request; I want to be on your side

Please open the door you closed.

6. Mind, Heart and Soul

Mind is restless

Every situation is turning on the adverse side

Hey, life again has thrown the most challenging ball to be played

Wants me to keep esteem to great heights

The soul is in a search for the real meaning in life

Time again strikes as a sharp knife

Fear, anxiety, and depression are its tactics to create a plight

Oh, my heart is full of positive and negative vibes

Assuring me, Defeat it

It is just a fight; your future is bright.

7. Oh God, I Was A Child

Today, I am on my death bed, counting my breath.

Memories of mistakes made as a child came to my mind

In prayer for regret, my heart said

Oh God, I was a child

I used to run after butterflies

Catching and caging them was a delight

I kept orange, red, and yellow

Unexpectedly Yellow one died

In guilt, I made a grave for her according to her size

In prayer for regret, my heart said

Oh God, I was a child

Fondness for flowers was my weakness

Roses, Lilies, and Jasmine were the best

Their smell blossomed into my mind

I plugged them in at night

In prayer for regret, my heart said

Oh God, I was a child

Pigeons, Nightingales, and Sparrows, were the birds to make my day

Their nest on trees full of leaves and grasses used to make me amazed

In curiosity, I took one sparrow's egg from her nest

I felt bad

In prayer for regret, my heart said

Oh God, I was a child

8. Soulmate

Somebody touched my soul with his love and positive energy
I wanted to erase his memories but found
He was my soulmate
Being apart from him, we will not be together in this life
Ocean of love brought tears to my eyes
Made me realize
He was my soulmate
Having faith in the force of the law of attraction
I want to have a glimpse of his soul in that heaven
Where I found
He was my soulmate
As souls are the little pieces of God, so we may be
From my little part to his, I want to shower divine energy
As in my prayers, I realize
He was my soulmate

9. Imperfections

Beauty lies in making corrections
When I tried to explore my inadequate life
I had a great fight
Found my perfect people left me for no reason
Hey, imperfect people were by my side in every tough season
Damn, it requires an appreciation
Life is beautiful to experience its faulty directions
Inexact timings teach you to learn exact lessons
Ignore the insufficiencies to maintain sufficient relations
The world is a fantastic place for celebration
Live a great life with perfect imperfections
It will give you motivation for outstanding creations.

10. A Broken Soul with Two Faces

Lonely was she in her inner world

She was deprived of love and trust

Living with a smile was necessary to make the connected people feel as usual.

Hey, she was the broken soul with two faces

Her real face had a privacy

It was full of depression and anxiety

Her loved ones left her forever; it was an irony.

She was scattered and clattered miserably.

She tried to look calm and full of compassion as she wanted to make the people associated with her life comfortable.

She was the broken spirit with two faces

Memories of the one she loved wholeheartedly

It made her sometimes pale, certainly

But she had no choice but to pretend a composite and happy life

So those people surrounding her can live blissfully

She was the broken soul with two faces

Exhausted, she was by show-off with her primary face

But the mirror had an idea of how isolated she was universally

She felt secure with her own emotions as no one needed an explanation

This was her genuine face which was secondary

Hey, she was a broken soul with two faces.

11. Twinkle of Your Love

I always felt a lack of contentment,

My life was blur.

But, your existence made me audacious and diminished my fear.

Hey, Your presence is blissful; now I am clear.

You are the star of my life, and I am the twinkle of your love smiling and blushing in every sphere.

I was always misunderstood, which made me disappear

Your tight warm hug made me believe in self-reliance

Hey, our connection is peaceful.

You are the bright star of my life. I am the twinkle of your love; it made me reappear.

I had many good traits, but people around me discouraged

Your kiss on my forehead made me believe in my powers

Hey, your presence is joyful.

You are the star like a divine messenger showering the shine. I am twinkle of your love with courage I gathered, and I am ready to fly with my feathers.

12. Transformation

From a setting sun to a rising one

There is a transformation of darkness into shine

From the feeling of being anxious to fearless, one

From being agitated to confident, one

There is a journey of transformation from tenacity to the vivacity

From a teary eye to blushing a smile

From devastating suffering to countless reasons to love life

There is a transformation of the painful past into hope of beautiful tomorrow

From being in a cage of own thoughts to the breaking of its pattern

Change from being sensitive to inevitably learning control over emotions

It leads to the indispensable transformation from pessimistic to optimistic person

This phase of conversion is of the slow movement

Hold the conviction at this pace of transformation

It will turn you into a superhuman.

13. Conviction

I am a shattered soul with no direction

Silence is there in my internal existence.

Loud is your voice asking me to hold a belief as things are hard to handle

Endless testing times are creeping into my world

Trust in your write-up for this life is indispensable to prove me a fortunate person.

I am sure your twist and turn will make me a fighter upfront

In every human providing me a helping hand, I find your connection

I am a broken soul deep down, losing a positive temperament

But in my consciousness, your loud voice asks me to hold conviction though things are hard to handle

Our bond is lovely and universally acceptable

In my loud cry, your silence shows me a way to be confident

Divine is your name who always wipes my tears with blessings that transform me into brave.

A rising, loud voice of uncertainty asks me to hold conviction; hard things are not everlasting to handle.

14. Human Relationships

A query always arises in my mind
Why do people change with time?
Convenience and self-motive are the traits in their prime
Care and love are taken for granted
Why whom we love wholeheartedly are not by our side?
This query always arises in my mind
Life gives few chances for its chapters to revise
Indeed, relations are complex when self-respect needs to be paid a price
Perhaps, these bonds are the hardest to understand
Significantly love is the foundation that makes them bright
Why the unpredictable goodbyes are unpleasant and full of inconvenient surprise?
This query always arises in my mind.
Clinging and holding a rusted relationship for sake of proving us right
Never leads to the future of togetherness keeps us haunted better to realize
Human relations are losing vivacity; no one wants to compromise
Misconceptions and assumptions are breaking them wide

Why does every second person have the same story and experience?

Abruptly, this query always arises in my mind.

15. Colour Box

Graceful was my childhood life.

Once my mother bought a Colour box, to my delight.

I made scenery of my imagination; the hut of my drawing was peaceful, and the rising sun between the mountains was full of pride.

I loved to draw the clown; his round face had a joyful smile without sight of plight.

I also drew various flowers. Pink and orange were the colour of my choice, making them bright.

My finger painting was beautiful; I felt glorified

The sketch of the rainbow had once a mismatch of colours, but no one was able to recognize it.

The blue was the colour I usually used to fill in stars, but there was a glittering silver colour in the box, to my surprise.

I used sketch pens for creating borders.

Crayons gave gloss to my art as combinations were in orders

But My crush for painting colour was amazingly high.

Graceful was my childhood life.

Once my mother bought a Colour Box to my delight.

16. Scattered Pieces

She fainted and was shattered, as she was seen with doubts though wholeheartedly was her sacrifice.

Aggression and fear were the feelings through which her inner world was distracted because she was considered a tool to fulfil selfish motives by the people in her life.

Broken were the pieces of her soul. The world made her pay the price.

Once there was love in her heart, and the smile on her face was bright.

But soon, her wish to live a beautiful life vanished; loud was her cry.

Trust and loyalty to her were considered pretentious by the shallow people in her life.

Broken was her soul into pieces; the world of misconceptions snatched her pride.

She is living by gathering the pieces of her broken soul. It is her immense try.

Magnetic is her connection with the divine. Each piece of her scattered soul is being given strength by the universe, which is a blessing in disguise.

17. Belief

The universe is full of galaxies.

Connected magnificently gives me strength and hope to hold a belief

Everything would be fine; don't get frozen.

The aggregation of past events made me think that nothing good would happen to lead me to aggression.

But the shining stars in the sky give me the power to believe your stage is waiting for you to move the mountains with determination. You will rock on your show. So be awake, don't sleep.

I was startled to notice my loved ones who wanted me to let down sympathy and love were not on the ground.

My thinking turned to be the victim crying out for wounds without sound.

Watching up in the sky birds flying with their feather made my caged soul hold the belief.

It's a time play. Keep the focus on your vision world will see your victory one or the other day. Don't act like a creep.

I know there is more darkness in my life, but every sunrise persuades me to hold a belief that there is a profound connection with the divine. It will guide you to the path of peace.

18. I Set My Heart on Fire

Your deep love for me was imaginary.
We are the characters of life's play, holding a view of exploratory
The more I try to understand your mindset, genuinely
I learn to become a visionary
Hey, I set my heart on fire by loving you amazingly
The less we communicate, the more our love gets enhanced with integrity
I find myself to be your critic in specific ways, surprisingly
But my love for you is like the silence of the deep eternal sea
It's noiseless but as much more most pleasing way to convey my care, outstandingly
Hey, I set my heart on fire by loving you amazingly
I wish I could experience life with you in reality
Our concern is not going to fade away it, certainly
What lures me a lot is your quality thoughts and simplicity
Hey, I set my heart on fire by loving you amazingly.

19. Ph.D. Guide

Simple was this man, but his personality was vibrant and bright.

His love for applications and technologies made him complete his doctorates.

Hey, he was an eminent Ph.D. guide.

His techniques for visualizing models and their crystal-clear explanation won students' sight. His knowledge was exuberantly high.

Innovative teaching skills were his tools which made him respectful and outstandingly wise.

He was a professional who was known for his astonishing accomplishments side.

With the passing time, his progression was a hike.

Learning is a never-ending process; it's a universal truth, right.

Though he was the evaluator of the highest degree, his deep grounded ethics were his insight.

Profoundly bounded was his love for books that before leaving this world, he read pages of modernisation.And books were scarred where his body laid.

His loss was irreversible; many cried.

Hey, he was an eminent Ph.D. guide.

20. Journey of My Flight

With low esteem, I was searching for a way to fight.

Duties and responsibilities were making me pale and white

Then a beautiful soul came into my life

Its motive was to make me rise

Shattered, clattered I was, the divine soul was able to recognize without utterance from my side.

The heavenly soul was the blessing in disguise

It helped me to improve from my roots

Thankfully I met myself was lost in worldly matters; I was not mine.

I had fallen and was unable to accept challenges.

It showed me that I have immense power to fly. And, it's a matter of learning and revising.

My tenacity was running downside.

Great soul reminded me of my goals as it believed my calibre was high

My journey on my flight was fascinating as the glad soul was my guide.

21. Havoc

In want of tranquillity, I am losing the vivacity of life

The core of responsibility is making it black and white

Mood swings, complaints, and inabilities to cope are damaging my bright side

Who is to blame for the present predicament? I have no clues. Hey, I am not wise

Shall I accept the pain, or I run away from the game

It is hard to decide

In the world of aspirations devoid of ethics, there is no tenacity to fly

There are countless opportunities to explore why I am turning insane

Whatever efforts I am putting is in vain

Is this a result of past evil deeds or a glitch of my emasculated density?

Confusion prevails on all the sides

I am losing the vivacity to rise.

22. Things Will Never Be Alright

Nothing seems to be alright.

A world of perseverance requires immense patience

It will lead you to a great height

Let the people who create hindrance in your life

Watch the success as they won't see your situation full of the plight

The vivacity of living a life is in its everyday fight

You will roll and mould it in gold

Problems are fire will once turn you bright

Your dear ones will never support you; they will accuse you of making a decision that was never right.

Let the tears in your eyes for unfortunate happenings be the pillar for your victorious flight.

Repercussions are not always positive failure is a ladder for rising in the sky.

Accomplish your dreams; your inner voice is the divine's aid for advice

Reckon it will prove you wise

Embrace your struggles as they will pay you a fortunate prize

23. Fades

Life keeps on moving in its phase.

The vitality of those things changes, which were once immensely chased

Exemplary is this perceived notion as, in reality, every, thing gets fades

Emotions have an enormous impact to create a great bond in any case

Time plays an evolutionary role, passing with it. Every connection fades

Memories of loved ones make our past always awake

Thinking about them, we shed tears with wiping off their remembrance. Our sentiment gets fades

The vision fades with age colour and energy of the body fades

Rudimentary is this process. Nothing can take its place

People have an altercation with opinions to win. They fight and adopt devious ways

But nothing remains at its pace living miserably, and their entity gets fades

Nostalgic is a keyword denoted to a past image

Everything is inconstant; a recollection of them becomes arduous their imagination gets fades

Craving for love is indispensable for human race

Pivotal is its role in every stage

Hey, life is a long journey love is a unique feeling which flows from the divine's grace

Don't let apathy and annoyance turn it into fades.

24. Silent Battle

My world is turning dynamic as the days pass by

The more I explore, the I become strong and wise

The combat zone of life is darker than bright

Sometimes it is blissful to be own; no two ways to follow a divine's flight

Others perceive my actions as traits of arrogance and pride

Non-adjustment towards their expectations brings a heavy price

Hey, there is always a silent battle that creates chaos and makes me wise

Self-doubt sometimes poses a situation of the plight

Why do society's rules and perceptions draw a way to live a life?

Constantly a questionable thing in mind arise.

It's a road that I always refuse to walk upon; I have my move to fight

The more I listen to my soul, I feel contented, and it motivates me to rise

Some connected people think my route and style will lead to the downside

Sadly, distraction and disturbance are the sights

Sometimes it forms havoc in thoughts, what is right and wrong. I can't visualize

But my true nature expression creates inner harmony, and self-transparency is eminently prioritized

Hey, there is always a silent battle that creates chaos and makes me wise.

25. Twin Flame

Empty was my world

Living a life without a smile, disheartened I was with life's curls

Your entry made me a person to think beyond the limits set by the world

You are my reflection who succours me in connecting with self-beauty

I remain intact; so soulful is this ritual designed by the universe

The beautiful relationship we have is crystal and clear

Our fights and concern help in digging a little deeper into tranquillity

Love, a profound bond, makes it easy to resolve unresolved mysteries

We are two different physical bodies, still one soul

How unique is the creation of a creator?

We are part of a split soul that keeps our hold

Our intense partnership is more valuable than diamond, pearl, and gold

Chasing each other gives us reason to run towards our spiritual goal

Fantabulous is our unbreakable connection where silence plays a significant role

Mutual rejection and persuasion lead to the reunion

We are part of fear, suffering, and isolation from many past lives which were not in our control

Let's reunite as our alignment will assemble us in the divine soul

Hey, you are my twin flame. I want to rejoice in our conscious energy as we are mirror souls.

26. No Point to Return Back

Crucial was the point

Reversal may lead to a clash

Tried harder to deal with every context

But losing vivacity was an always a setback

Mind trembled and sneered.

There is no point in returning back.

Insecurities and confounded feelings were unwanted guests

Perseverance and courage's roleplay were best

Some called it Ego; for others, it sounded like a stubborn act

A heart desired to explore life on its own rules with zeal and zest

It was pointless to return back

According to some, setting own direction in madness is a hazardous step

But, walking on it turned up wonderfully and brought contentment; I took a soulful breath

Tenacity and self-understanding were holding inevitable quest

Hey, I kept on moving forward as there was no point in returning back

27. A Sound of Silence

Beautiful noise, a profound connection

Myriad unsaid words have an eminent impression. A sound of silence has many things to adjourn, directing towards the creation of an unleashed relation.

Unlearned lessons to be learned

Quietness is a way of enhancing our unbreakable bond gracefully under the sun.

Hey, it is not a race to run. Instead, patience is a keyword for our anxiety to burn.

A sound of silence turns our attachment into admiration

Our fights convert into deep conversations

Unresolved conflicts switch to our concern

Extinguishment of argument leads toward each other's inclination.

Our Heartfelt love requires appreciation.

A sound silence keeps awake our souls' interrelation.

28. Virus Outbreak

Deadly is the strain

There is no choice but to bargain

Fear and anxiety rule the mind making it difficult peace to maintain

Scarcity is at its peak shortage of oxygen, vaccine, and medical assistance are publics plead

The world is turning into a danger zone only option is to stay at home

Near and dear ones are not taking a moment to say the last goodbye

Their cremation ceremonies have remained unattended; it is a miserable plight

Doctors are becoming helpless and mentally sick

The ones who were looked upon as earthly gods are unstable and in trauma as the virus has made a grip

Road and streets are empty, clean, and refined; only dogs and cows are roaming for their bread and wine

The Voice of the hospital plane is heard the whole day and night.

God knows who is turning to be healthy and who will be on the last flight.

Financial constraints, emotional war, and health deterioration are a pandemic sight.

Leaders are trolled for their inability to capture this hike.

A divine force with a universal existence

wants people to learn the lesson of equality and respect for humankind.

Love everyone, be scrupulous, as God is not in temples and monuments; it's in the human soul. Be kind.

Updates happening across the globe keep people mentally disturbed and anxious. Hey, it's time I came close to nature.

As meditation and connection with breath were inevitable to be out of perilous

Prayers and well-being wish brought people together and made them wise.

Health holds an enormous role; please take care. Its proper function is only survival device

Wearing a mask is a compulsion, and sanitization of hands at every point is crucial.

Share the optimistic hope with everyone and abstain from virulent thoughts, as solidarity is only key to winning this epidemic fight

29. Soul Sister

My words, your sentences

My emotions, your understanding

My love, your arguments. Behind every fight, our care is hidden

My pains and negative attitude, your positive outlook

My temperament to see the downside, your motivation to hold hope and rise

Your smile is priceless and full of pride. It brings vivacity to my eyes

My imagination and your courage to turn it into reality, you are wise

Contrast is our divine connection that does not need any communication

I wonder if we aren't brother and sister, even with no blood relation. Hey, it is alright

Still, our bond is robust and keeps us alive by holding wisdom

Nostalgic, I feel thinking about the spent moments in the rhythm

You have the tenacity to climb high won't allow you to collapse; I will be your support system

You are my soul, sister, an inevitable part of my kingdom.

30. Not Taking A Moment To Say Goodbye

Our bond was unbreakable

You were the spark of my eyes

I rejoiced every moment I spent with you

Nothing was to my delight

Your everyday care led to my enhancement

It was certainly a pride

My happiness was always your incessant effort

Your presence resembled a surrounded rainbow, bright

Your vibration emitted positive vibes that made me rise

Unfortunately, you left me forever. Shattered, I was massively, and I cried.

Frustration, Distraction was the consequences of your grievance

Certainly, was lost in your remembrance. You were consistently on my side

Profound was our relation, and no one can take your place in this life

Broken, shaken my heart in disappointment, questions,

Why didn't you hold my hand at that moment to say the last goodbye?

31. Move On

They say to live a peaceful life, move on from the past.
Past is past. Its remembrance brings tears and pain.
But my heart asked my brain.
How can I move on? It is my past.

Life is full of ups and downs.
Some happenings are sweet, and some are sour.
In mine, an account of sour may be vast.
My heart, in sadness, mourned, said
How can I move on? It is my past.

Counting of difficulties, suffering, and agony was high.
It seemed laughter, love, and happiness for me were denied.
My heart shattered, remembered.
How can I move on? It is my past.

My loved ones left me forever.
Life taught me their non-existence would be forever.
My heart in attachment shouted.
How can I move on? It is my past.

Moving On is the key to happiness.
But for me, memories of the past are full of greatness.
My past directs my dark present.
Wind of these thoughts brought speedy rain to my heart.
The tears that glittered in my eye made me realize.
How can I move on? It is my past though it has passed.

32. Light Lamp

Once you were my companion, your light made me amazed.

During the time of my adversity, you gave me hope of ray.

In this world of advanced technology, where things are at a single-finger play

Nature showed its power disaster of the earthquake made my life fierce.

Darkness was only in my space remittance of your light had the potential to weigh

My broken heart with deep resentment, along with memories of a lost dear one, was like pointed blades

Your illumination made me focus on my longways

Shattered, scattered, and ruptured, my world was at stake.

Your sparkling light made me attain goals; I embrace

We had a vigorous rapport throughout nights for maths practice, science diagrams, or any learning; you were my associate

I cherish our linkage. You helped me climb up.

Those tough times have accustomed me to being awake

Years passed, and my world changed

Still, I have a profound admiration for you, my workmate.

33. Last Breath

The capture of my whole life is in front of my eyes
It's a story of my last breath, which was at a hike
I regretted for my complaining mode
Life is blissful, and it's not a joke
The consciousness of truth made my soul evoke
It's a story of my last breath; nothing is in store
My world always revolved around logic and reasoning
Altercations for right and wrong were at large part of thought forming
Why I judged people immensely, my values were diminishing
It's a story of my last breath,
it was the divine's blessing.
I had an option to embrace the life's uncertainty
It was the profound exposure to the integrity
But I keenly made an effort to find the safe side
Oh, it was not the right decision; I paid the price
Shall I endure my mortal state or else I leave my body in agony, was the only choice I had to make
My soul strived hard; it envisaged
Hey, existence in the world is arduous.

Don't lament, be scrupulous.

Still, you have a chance to cherish the vivacity of life

It's a story of my last breath; I wish I could be alive.

34. A Happy Land

I want to be with you on that land, where my love for you gets enhanced

Where your support takes away my fears prevalent,

Where our fights get resolved within seconds,

I want to be with you in that happy land.

Where my insecurities for you turn into tranquillity and contentment, immensely loving you brings confidence

Where I can listen to your heartbeats expecting care from my end, nothing to say more but with a cheerful temperament,

I want to be with you in that happy land.

Where our unbreakable bond augments faith in the divine's play for building our fantastic connection,

Life is full of adversities and ominous circumstances, sometimes not offering a second chance for betterment.

Grievously we can't be together forever in that happy land.

35. Cosmic Connection

Your and my universal connection is in gaze

I don't know your identity.

Indeed, no one can take your holy place.

To my surprise, as an inner voice or as intuition, you stipulate

Amid adversity, like a mystical voice, you ask me to hold on to faith

In the form of a friend, you persuade my conscious not to alleviate

Your appearance as courage makes my fears fade

An instinct you may be, who guides me to explore life, profoundly I am amazed.

As divine energy, you eliminate all illusions about existence and proffer truth at any stake.

You are supernatural power or my guardian angel

Still not explicit about our linkage

Striving incessantly to create a strong bond with you

As this unbreakable connection makes my concise exquisitely awake

36. Happiness A Myth

The world is an experienced land
Moments and memories are its gist
People with ego and arrogance want to feel bliss
Suffering and pain they wish under a grip
Hey, Happiness is a myth.
Live life with controlled emotions; don't slip
The reaction makes blenders if made quick
Don't run from the situation
Face it with zeal in a single click
Rest Is your wish
But do remember
Happiness is just a myth.

37. Walk Without A Soul

Enlightenment and everlasting happiness are traits of pure souls

I wonder why people walk without souls

There is no empathy for others' suffering

Selfish motives are the reasons for serving

No room for faith and trust in life

Lies and Sins are rising to great heights

I wonder why people walk without souls.

The creditability of words is replaced by money

Simplicity and innocence are considered funny

Status is the base for every deal

What is truth in mind no one reveals

Ego and jealousy are the traits of people without souls

I, too, am one of them.

Becoming indifferent to things for me was not in my control

I walk without a soul.

38. Dreamful Life

Many dreams, my wings are ready to fly

Want to climb high to touch the sky.

Constraints and responsibilities have no place in hijacking my flight

To the destiny of the wonderful land of dreams will surely reach

By making beautiful my journey called life

39. A Man with Advice

A man with advice had a dark side

His life full of misfortunes made him wise

The journey of his existence was pale and full of plight

A man with advice had a dark side.

With a broken heart, persistent efforts to climb were an excellent sign

Misconceptions and unacceptance of the world were the secrets to his shine

A man with advice once cried because he had a dark side

Today he aspires me to touch the sky

His pleasing smile motivates me to rise

Perseverance and self-assurance are the only words in his guide

A man who once had a dark side gave me honest advice, life is full of compromise

www.ingramcontent.com/pod-product-compliance
Ingram Content Group UK Ltd.
Pitfield, Milton Keynes, MK11 3LW, UK
UKHW040013200726
13854UKWH00001B/174

9 789356 284166